Healthy 7 Habits for Teens

SIMPLE STEPS FOR A HEALTHIER AND BALANCED LIFE

PETER MAC

....

....

....

....

....

....

....

....

Contents

Dedicated to all teens and young-adults

INTRODUCTION

Welcome to "Seven Healthy Habits for Teens"!

As a teenager, you are at an exciting and transforming moment in your life. You are learning, growing, and gaining new skills and abilities that will build the foundation for your future. And while there are many things to be enthusiastic about, there are also plenty of problems and stresses that come with being a teenager. That's where this book comes in.

In "Seven Healthy Behaviors for Teens," we'll take a look at seven simple, but powerful habits that can help you improve your physical and mental health, boost your energy and focus, and build a more balanced and satisfying life. From eating a healthy, balanced diet and exercising frequently, to getting enough sleep and managing stress, these habits can help you feel your best and set you up for success in school and in life.

Whether you are wanting to improve your overall health and well-being, or you want to tackle specific health issues or obstacles, "Seven Healthy Habits for Teens" is the appropriate guide. With clear, step-by-step directions and plenty of tips and tricks, this book makes it easy to adopt healthy behaviors and achieve permanent improvements.

So let's get started! In the pages that follow, we'll explore each of the seven healthy habits in detail and show you how to implement them into your life. Are you ready to make a good change and take control of your health and well-being? Let's do it!

Chapter 1

Exercises

Regular physical exercise is an important aspect of sustaining excellent physical health and emotional well-being. Regular physical activity can assist to improve cardiovascular fitness, strengthen bones and muscles, and minimize the risk of chronic diseases such as obesity, diabetes, and heart disease. It can also help to promote mental health by reducing stress, enhancing mood, and increasing self-esteem.

There are many other sorts of exercise that can be beneficial, including activities such as jogging, swimming, cycling, and team sports. The type of exercise you pick will depend on your specific tastes and physical level. It is vital to find activities that you enjoy, as this will make it more likely that you will persist with the fitness schedule.

For best health advantages, it is advised that adults and teens aim for at least 60 minutes of moderate to intense physical activity each day. This can be achieved by a combination of moderate-intensity activities such as brisk walking or dancing, and vigorous-intensity activities such as running or soccer. It is also vital to add activities that build muscles at least twice a week.

Exercise is an important aspect of sustaining excellent physical and emotional well-being, and it is something that everybody can do. By making it a regular part of your routine, you can experience the many benefits of physical activity and improve your overall health and happiness.

QUOTE

- ❖ "Physical fitness is not only one of the most important keys to a healthy body, it is the basis of dynamic and creative intellectual activity." - John F. Kennedy

- ❖ "Exercise is king. Nutrition is queen. Put them together and you've got a kingdom." - Jack LaLanne

- ❖ "Exercise is a keystone habit that triggers widespread change. Exercise is not just about looking better. Exercise can make you feel better, think clearer, and sleep better." - Charles Duhigg

- ❖ "Exercise is the miracle cure we've always had, but for too long we've neglected to take our recommended dose." - Dr. Jordan Metzl

❖ "Exercise is not just about going to the gym. It is about the choices you make every day to live a healthy lifestyle." - Michelle Obama

These quotes highlight the many benefits of exercise, from improving physical health to boosting mental clarity and creativity. Regular physical activity is essential for maintaining good health and well-being, and it is something that anyone can do. By making exercise a part of your daily routine, you can enjoy the many benefits it has to offer and improve your overall quality of life.

Chapter 2

Adequate Sleep

Adequate sleep is crucial for good physical and mental performance in teens, as well as in adults. Sleep is vital for a number of reasons, including:

Physical health: During sleep, the body has an opportunity to repair and renew cells, tissues, and organs. Adequate sleep is also vital for keeping a healthy immune system and for regulating weight.

Mental health: Sleep is vital for maintaining healthy mental health. It helps to boost mood, reduce stress, and increase cognitive function, particularly memory and learning.

Development: During the adolescent years, the brain undergoes tremendous development and maturity, and sleep plays a crucial role in this process. Adequate sleep is needed for appropriate brain growth and function.

Despite the significance of sleep, many teens struggle to obtain enough of it.

According to the National Sleep Foundation, kids need between 8-10 hours of sleep per night, however many teens do not get this much sleep. This can have detrimental implications for their physical and emotional health, as well as their academic achievement.

Quotes

- ❖ "Sleep is the best meditation." - Dalai Lama

- ❖ "I think sleep is so important. I think it's one of the best things you can do for your body." - Jennifer Aniston

- ❖ "Sleep is the most powerful productivity hack. I always tell people that the reason I'm able to do so much is that I'm well-rested." - Tim Ferriss

- ❖ "The secret of health for both mind and body is not to mourn for the past, worry about the future, or anticipate troubles, but to live in the present moment wisely and earnestly." – Buddha

- ❖ "Sleep is the golden chain that ties health and our bodies together." - Thomas Dekker

These quotes highlight the many benefits of sleep and the importance of getting enough of it. By prioritizing sleep and making it a priority, teens can improve their physical and mental health and function at their best.

It is important for teens to create a sleep-friendly environment, establish a consistent sleep routine, and limit exposure to screens and other distractions before bedtime in order to get the sleep they need.

In conclusion, adequate sleep is essential for proper physical and mental functioning in teens. It is important for teens to prioritize sleep and make it a part of their daily routine in order to enjoy the many benefits it has to offer. By getting enough sleep, teens can improve their physical and mental health, boost their cognitive function and academic performance, and live their best lives.

Chapter 3

Eating A Balanced Diet

Eating a nutritious, balanced diet is vital for sustaining good physical health in teens, as much as in adults. A healthy diet provides the body with the nutrition it needs to function correctly and to sustain excellent health. It can assist to enhance energy levels, stimulate the immune system, and minimize the risk of chronic diseases like as obesity, diabetes, and heart disease.

A healthy, balanced diet for teens should include a range of foods from all food groups, including:

Fruits and vegetables: These give critical vitamins, minerals, and fiber, and should make up a major component of the diet. Aim for at least 5 servings of fruits and vegetables per day.

Whole grains: These include foods such as whole grain bread, rice, and pasta, and give key nutrients such as fiber, B vitamins, and iron. Choose whole grain choices wherever possible.

Lean proteins: These include foods such as chicken, fish, beans, and tofu, and supply critical nutrients such as protein, iron, and zinc. Aim for at least 2 servings of protein per day.

Dairy: Dairy products such as milk, cheese, and yogurt give vital nutrients such as calcium, protein, and vitamin D. Aim for at least 3 servings of dairy every day.

It is also crucial to minimize intake of bad foods such as processed and sugary foods, which can contribute to poor health and weight gain.

By eating a healthy, balanced diet, teens can retain good physical health and enjoy the numerous benefits it has to offer. It is crucial for teens to be attentive of their eating habits and to make healthy choices whenever possible.

Quotes

- ❖ "Let food be thy medicine and medicine be thy food." – Hippocrates

- ❖ "You are what you eat, so don't be fast, cheap, easy, or fake." – Anonymous

- ❖ "Eating is a necessity, but cooking is an art." - William Shakespeare

- ❖ "Eating healthy is not about strict dietary limitations, staying unrealistically thin, or depriving yourself of the foods you love. Rather, it's about feeling great, having more energy, improving your health, and boosting your mood." - Michelle Obama

- ❖ "The food you eat can be either the safest and most powerful form of medicine or the slowest form of poison." - Ann Wigmore

These quotes highlight the importance of making healthy food choices and the impact that diet can have on overall health and well-being. By eating a healthy, balanced diet, teens can maintain good physical health and enjoy the many benefits it has to offer. It is important for teens to be mindful of their eating habits and to make healthy choices whenever possible.

Chapter 4

Hydration

Hydration is a crucial aspect of maintaining excellent physical health and well-being. Water is vital for many of the body's activities, including maintaining body temperature, carrying nutrients and oxygen to cells, and eliminating waste and toxins from the body. It is crucial to drink enough water throughout the day to stay hydrated and support these essential functions.

There are several benefits to keeping sufficient hydration, including:

Improved physical performance: Proper hydration is vital for physical performance, especially during exercise. It helps to maintain energy levels and prevent weariness, and it can also assist to improve endurance and minimize the danger of muscle cramps.

Better brain function: Adequate hydration is vital for sustaining excellent cognitive function, including concentration, memory, and mood.

Dehydration can lead to weariness, irritation, and difficulties concentrating.

Healthy skin: Water is crucial for maintaining healthy skin. It helps to keep the skin hydrated and firm, and it can also help to lessen the appearance of wrinkles and fine lines.

Improved digestion: Water is vital for efficient digestion and the absorption of nutrients from food. It helps to keep the digestive tract running normally and can assist to prevent constipation.

Weight control: Drinking water can aid to promote weight management attempts by helping to fill the stomach and lower appetite. It can also aid to flush out extra toxins and waste from the body.

It is crucial for teens to drink enough water throughout the day to remain hydrated and enjoy the many benefits of adequate hydration. The American Academy of Pediatrics recommended that teens drink at least 8-10 glasses of water every day.

Quotes

- ❖ "Drink lots of water. Your skin will thank you." - Jennifer Aniston

- ❖ "Water is the driving force of all nature." - Leonardo da Vinci
- ❖ "You're not sick, you're thirsty. Don't treat thirst with medication." - F. Batmanghelidj

- ❖ "Hydration is key to a healthy body." - Jillian Michaels

- ❖ "Drink plenty of water. Water is the elixir of life." - Tony Robbins

Chapter 5

Effective Time Managemment

Effective time management is a vital ability for adolescents to master in order to be successful in school and in other aspects of life. It entails creating goals, prioritizing work, and organizing and managing time in order to achieve tasks and meet deadlines. Here is some content about successful time management for teens, with extra quotes from prominent persons on the subject:

Set clear goals: To manage your time successfully, it is necessary to have a clear picture of what you want to accomplish. This can allow you to prioritize chores and focus your efforts on the most critical things.

Make a schedule: A timetable can enable you to arrange your time and keep track of your responsibilities and commitments. It can also allow you to prevent overbooking or double-booking yourself, and to manage your time more effectively.

Prioritize tasks: Not all tasks are created equal, and it is vital to prioritize tasks depending on their relevance and urgency. This can allow you to focus your attention on the most critical things and to manage your time more efficiently.

Use time management tools: There are several tools available to help you manage your time more successfully, including calendars, to-do lists, and time management applications. These tools can enable you to keep track of your responsibilities and commitments, and to stay organized and on track.

<u>Learn to say no:</u> It is crucial to be judicious about the duties and responsibilities you take on, and to be willing to say no when necessary. This can allow you to manage your time more effectively and to avoid overdoing yourself.

Quotes

- ❖ "Time management is an act or process of planning and exercising conscious control over the amount of time spent on specific activities, especially to increase effectiveness, efficiency, and productivity." – Wikipedia

- ❖ "The two most powerful warriors are patience and time." - Leo Tolstoy

- ❖ "Time management is really a misnomer; the challenge is not to manage time, but to manage ourselves." - Stephen Covey

- ❖ "Lost wealth may be replaced by industry, lost knowledge by study, lost health by temperance or medicine, but lost time is gone forever." - Samuel Smiles

- ❖ "Your time is limited, don't waste it living someone else's life." - Steve Jobs

These quotes highlight the importance of managing your time effectively and the role that self-management plays in this process. By setting goals, making a schedule, prioritizing tasks, and using time management tools, teens can learn to manage their time more effectively and accomplish more in less time.

It is also important to be selective about the tasks and commitments you take on and to learn to say no when necessary in order to avoid overloading yourself. By developing effective time management skills, teens can increase their effectiveness, efficiency, and productivity, and set themselves up for

success in school and in other areas of
life.

Chapter 6

Stress Management

Stress is a common part of life and it can be produced by a multitude of circumstances, including school, relationships, and personal concerns. While some stress can be useful and assist to inspire and focus us, too much stress can be destructive to our physical and mental health. It is crucial for kids to learn how to manage stress in a healthy way in order to preserve good physical and mental well-being.

Here are some ways for controlling stress:

Identify the sources of stress: The first step in managing stress is to identify the sources of stress in your life. This can enable you to understand what is causing your stress and to build methods for managing these causes of stress.

Learn to relax: Relaxation techniques, such as deep breathing, meditation, and progressive muscle relaxation, can assist to reduce stress and enhance general well-being. Taking time to rest and unwind can be a crucial element of stress management.

Exercise regularly: Regular physical activity can assist to alleviate stress and promote mental health. Exercise can assist to alleviate tension, boost mood, and increase self-esteem.

Eat a healthy, balanced diet: A good diet can help to improve general physical and mental health and can be an important aspect of stress management. Aim for a diet that includes a range of fruits, vegetables, whole grains, lean proteins, and healthy fats.

Get enough sleep: Adequate sleep is crucial for optimal physical and mental health. Aim for at least 8-10 hours of sleep per night to help manage stress and preserve excellent health.

Connect with others: Building solid relationships with friends and family can be very rewarding. You most likely knew that this was coming. It is one of the most efficient techniques of dealing with stress building. Whether this is a friend, a family member or a psychotherapist, it doesn't matter in the slightest.

The only thing that matters is that you know someone that will listen to all of your concerns and offer you a shoulder for you to lay on in your times of need.

Regardless of who you are or what type of a person you think you are, you need to accept the fact that we all fall on our knees every now and again and need a pick-me-up. This has nothing to do with keeping your image or massaging that ego, it is a requirement.

Forget about being the "cool guy that doesn't need help" for a bit and worry about your sanity for once. Believe us when we tell you that this is no funny matter and that you'll have to deal with it sooner than later.

Quotes

- ❖ "Stress is nothing more than a socially acceptable form of mental illness." - Richard Carlson

- ❖ "The greatest weapon against stress is our ability to choose one thought over another." - William James

- ❖ "The greatest remedy for stress is self-expression." - Thomas Fuller

- ❖ "The best way to cope with stress is to prevent it." – Anonymous

- ❖ "The time to relax is when you don't have time for it." - Sydney J. Harris

These quotes highlight the importance of managing stress and the role that our thoughts and actions play in this process. By identifying the sources of stress, learning to relax, exercising regularly, eating a healthy diet, getting enough sleep, and connecting with others, teens can learn to manage stress in a healthy way and maintain good physical and mental well-being.

Chapter seven

Risky Behaviours

As a teen, you may encounter a lot of pressure and temptation to engage in harmful behaviors, but having a healthy life is all about choosing smart choices. It's crucial for kids to avoid risky habits like smoking, drinking alcohol, and using drugs since they can have major negative implications on their health and well-being.

Here are a few ways that teens can avoid harmful habits and maintain a healthy life:

Say no to drugs and alcohol: It may be tempting to try drugs or alcohol, especially when everyone else seems to be doing it, but these substances can have major negative implications on your physical and mental health. If you feel pushed to take drugs or alcohol, remember that it's alright to say no and to surround yourself with friends who appreciate your decision.

Using drugs can have devastating short-term and long-term impacts on the body and brain. Some substances can lead to addiction, which can have terrible effects for the individual and their loved ones. Drinking alcohol can impair judgment and coordination, which can lead to accidents and injuries. It can also increase the risk of acquiring health problems such as liver disease and some types of cancer.

Smoking can lead to major health concerns such as lung cancer, emphysema, and heart disease. It can also cause premature wrinkles, foul breath, and yellowed teeth.

Practice safe sex: It's crucial to protect yourself and your partner by using condoms and engaging in safe sexual practices. Not only can unprotected sex lead to unexpected pregnancies, but it can also put you at risk for sexually transmitted illnesses (STIs).

Wear a seatbelt: Wearing a seatbelt can save your life in the event of an automobile accident. Make careful to buckle up every time you get in a car, no matter how short the journey.

By following these recommendations, teens may make healthy decisions and avoid harmful activities. Remember, it's alright to seek for support if you're feeling overwhelmed or unclear about how to make healthy decisions. There are many tools available to support you on your road towards a healthy and meaningful life.

By avoiding these dangerous activities, you may help to protect their health and well-being and set yourself up for a bright and healthy future.

Quotes

- ❖ "The price of greatness is responsibility." - Winston Churchill

- ❖ "To be great is to be misunderstood." - Ralph Waldo Emerson

- ❖ "I can't change the direction of the wind, but I can adjust my sails to always reach my destination." - Jimmy Dean

- ❖ "The only true limitation is the one you set for yourself." - Roger Bannister

- ❖ "To be yourself in a world that is constantly trying to make you something else is the greatest accomplishment." - Ralph Waldo Emerson

- ❖ "The only person you should try to be better than is the person you were yesterday." - Anonymous

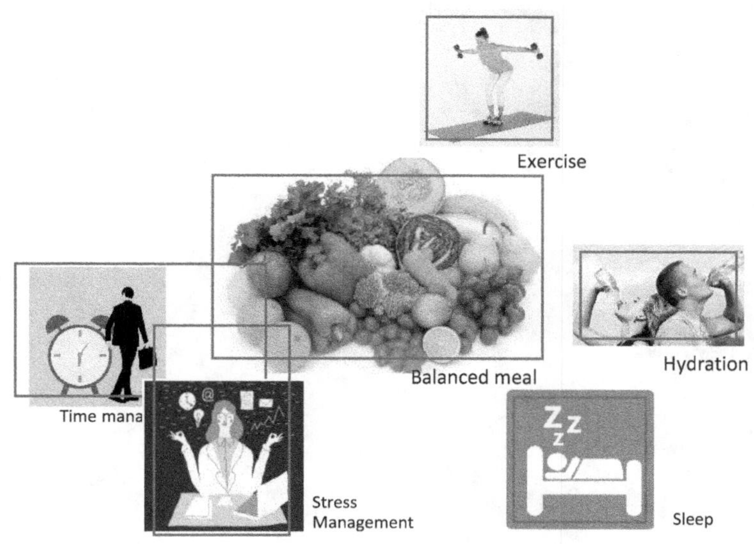

Exercise
Balanced meal
Hydration
Time mana
Stress
Management
Sleep